Quarantine with Rilke

poems by

Asnia Asim

Finishing Line Press
Georgetown, Kentucky

Quarantine with Rilke

Copyright © 2022 by Asnia Asim
ISBN 978-1-64662-794-3 First Edition
All rights reserved under International and Pan-American Copyright Conventions. No part of this book may be reproduced in any manner whatsoever without written permission from the publisher, except in the case of brief quotations embodied in critical articles and reviews.

ACKNOWLEDGMENTS

For this little book I owe a lot of love to some very special people:
My daughter, Larina, who came two months early and took our breath away.
My sister, Amina Asim, whose voice is my light.
Ami & Abu, for nourishing my love of language.
My Lebanese family: Tante and Uncle, Samer, Ali, Mohammad, Sara, Bana, and Joury.
My friends: Madiha, Fatima, Lama, Nazrana, Zunera, Alexia, Manoli, Christos, Stefania, Mathias, and Karen, for being there, for thoughtfully reading many of these poems, for cheerleading my solitude.
Michigan Quarterly Review and *Empathy Media Lab* for giving some of these poems a home.
E. Ethelbert Miller, for his generosity and guidance.
Diane Fishman, for showing me the strength within.
And finally, thanks to Finishing Line Press, for making this book happen.

Publisher: Leah Huete de Maines
Editor: Christen Kincaid
Cover Art: Lara Zankoul
Author Photo: Amika Gair Photography
Cover Design: Elizabeth Maines McCleavy

Order online: www.finishinglinepress.com
also available on amazon.com

Author inquiries and mail orders:
Finishing Line Press
PO Box 1626
Georgetown, Kentucky 40324
USA

Table of Contents

astronaut 1

city of (dis)quiet 2

a violent bloom 3

stay 5

portrait of the man upstairs 6

nightswimming 7

survivor's guilt 8

quench 9

the journey of words 11

horoscope 12

kindness 13

to silence 14

trees 15

portrait of woman in see-through blouse 16

alter ego 18

let me save you 20

against form 21

tease 22

wrong side of bed 23

autumn 24

wanderlust 25

afternoon sun 26

introvert 27

flirt 28

posture of embrace 29

nostos 30

For Ahmad,
who is home.

astronaut

Do you ever feel like
>you're on some far-flung asteroid, and you're looking down through a telescope, and around you, there is all this unharnessed cosmic beauty, and you want to channel it toward that middle-aged man you've caught through darkness in the circle of your lens, and you've been watching him for weeks, his dog and him, in his wifebeater loafing about, a lean sense of pleasure about his body, and in his idleness, something despairingly innocent, something delicate and important about the fact that he is after all, like you, some infinitesimal speck of dust, stuck to a pebble, spinning in the middle of infinity, and yet, you've kind of grown to like his unshaved face, and every morning his pathetic attempt to exercise his forgotten body, while far, far away, you are but a form, perhaps from the theory of forms, you are an idea, that might vaguely occur to him in the middle of a bath, or one night in the mirror, he might recognize you, startled, by the dazzling freedom of his irrelevance, by the fact that he is this tiny, tiny thing, sans purpose, sans consequence, happening in the fragrance of the shadow of a petal's intention to fall

Do you ever feel like that?

city of (dis)quiet

> "The world is quiet, and the silence is horrifying. I live alone, so I can only tell there are other human beings around from the occasional noises in the corridor."
> —Guo Jing, Wuhan China

O, the otherness of place has subsumed the city.

That other, quiet, kind of violence has invaded
its wings. A dog tied up somewhere

is barking her sorrow. Chaos is negotiating
with bodies: fevered temples, sweaty palms,

are swaying in lonesome rooms
that occasionally beep.

Between buildings a stillness keeps rising
from itself. Eagles fly low.

It's 3 am: church bells are cold.
That siren—coming or going? Flashing
in the distance.

When noise recedes, what returns is not
peace, but the deafening repetition
of silence.

a violent bloom

For too long he pursued it by capture.
The moon would welcome on its powdered skin
the foot of his ambition, his flag.
Or as he dove deep, submarined
his appetite's fragrance,
he wore out whales, god-like blue, until
they cried at him in his sleep.

Buildings he would design such
that they laid claim upon the sky:
raising them up even higher, swiftly, in days.
But then one day, the landscape,
overburdened by him,
began to breathe again
in the silent night of his absence.

Animals once wary of him, tiptoed
into his missing gaze, nibbling
on chestnut and grub,
and the ever-hounded pink lions
peered, trying to understand this impossible freedom,
birds of spring, as it bid them, flew vast,
they flew deep, and fruit, tempting
as it was to Eve, fell into it
on and on, with no one to eat.

And the myth that there once was a false god
—who knew how to take, and use,
and manipulate, but never give—
that rumor stirred no one.

Wait for how long?
Who should wait for his return?
Expect what from the vision of his mind?

Now he, who had forgotten the art of Stillness, sits far from himself—
the airport's colorless terminal
aloof around him, and in the hallway window
once again another emptiness, and later
from screens within screens:
voices discussing the incomprehensible,
but his heart, under his shirt
still beating to live,
wondering what, through the fragility of skin
could somehow betray him—his heart
wondering if time had finally passed its verdict:
that he had never known love.

For there is an end to doing,
an end to subverting mountains,
and stealing rivers.
And a world that is done in so thoroughly
longs for a violent bloom.

stay

Dear, who could not stay. Dear, I know you
twice: in your absence: your continuation,
multiform, diffuse.

The old man upstairs, who used to sell honey
and milk, he has taken to writing poetry.
I listen from my balcony. His voice still sounds
like the voice of a bearded man. But I am distracted

by that woman in her see-through blouse,
under the constant moon talking to her plants.
Her shoulders gleam in colors of sea, as if

reflecting verses of the poet unseen:

Beauty is nothing, he reads,
but the beginning of terror.

Angels seem to haunt him, too.

This night, terribly real. I could
go back inside and turn on the TV. Scatter
myself into images that trigger envy,

new appetites, occasional pity—a sense of divine impotence.

But I stay outside, knowing, that even springtime needs you.

Our neighbor's voice fades. Salt of stars liquifies in dawn.
On the empty wet road, a lone boy is running:
Away from? Toward—what?

But your image: stays. Incarnate, frail, full of self-respect.

portrait of the man upstairs

This thin, intimate ceiling. His time touching mine.
His daily routine fondling the margin of my dreams.

His shower's steam rolling through my walls:
I lay drenched in dry rain.

On my ceiling I can trace the stains of his cough.

Verses he reads out to stars become voyeurs,
sit on my balcony, watch me watch them.

Heroes of solitude, him and I. Parallel fields of mundane
blooming and unblossoming in between, until

he retires to sleep. And I slip back into the maze
of images within: this private arcade of moods

and missed beauty. Untethered, the heart's hunger reels,
desires permanence, to embody purity: to become

that soil in which tulips open, or that shade of blue
reserved for the sparrow's gaze. But then upstairs

he wakes, clears his throat, and pulls me back
into his routine.

We could be friends, him and I. I used to see him in the market.

Once, on the stairs I saw him looking for his keys, smelling
of cinnamon and smoke. His beard is God.

I want to make him laugh.

nightswimming

Waves release from you your

earth-bound privations—

    in an ether half-unknown, you hesitate.

    A larger sense of self emergent.

        This force of high seas, this will-bending

        groove. What is this joke? Around

            your insect frame, this play of

            mountainous water. And from the sky

                galaxies—irises of eternity—Why do they

                bring themselves to you, Nobody?

survivor's guilt

For days now, I have fed on loneliness, its dizzying
red fruit. My hands have become aware
of each other, my lips are warm and dry—this strange
late plum wine. There must be
an abundance of roses somewhere out there.

I lay here all day without you, relieved
from the abstractions of self-worth. But how to divert
the galaxies within?

This undergrowth of dry weeds,
wilderness of heart.

The bathroom mirror keeps drawing me in.
I watch my nudity float on the pale blue glass.

Nothing statuesque, reverential, about this.
I remain a fracture in time: delicate, sexual, cooked
in common blood.

I look older than I should.

I remember how the world gathered itself
away from you, too. And now,
this sweet, unbearable guilt.

I have outlived my love.

quench

Days pass, nothing happens.
Vacuous life bristles and burns.

Birds strike fruit,
figs split open on stones scorched in light,

this sexless monotony
paired with dense books,

being alive has taken
the density of concrete.

City lights blur in bands of heat.

Everyone I know longs for more sleep,

yet under this drowning and wakening,
beyond the comingling

of desire and disease, there is a glimmer

of perfumed linen, cheap wine restaurants,

crowded swimming pools, and beer gardens at night,

and the beauty of long earrings

in short hair, and of love

rising within us cold and free—

for beyond the dunes of waiting, there must be
a midnight pitilessly blue,

and a love that stoops down

to drink, a river that seeks the sea,

and someone to slake this thirst

stagnant and keen.

the journey of words

It could be said that my words
are members of a search party
I keep sending out for you.

They return from strange places:
from fields of stars, from the ruined bodies
of cities, even from the room next-door—
they return empty-handed but

altered, sounding different, wiser.
They come back smelling of snow,
of gunmetal, of your mother's
cupboard where she hid the tin of biscuits.

Words I send out for you return
with the gait of pilgrims.
Their sound tastes less of language,
more of sweat and pollen. They come

back bruised, but with a grasp
on autumn, and the shadows of jellyfish
in the Baltic Sea, and somehow, they
know too the sleeping place of Zeus.

They show but refuse to tell
where all the missing children are.
Warm to touch, they are smooth,
they fit quietly, without fuss

into the arc of your gloom.
Dissolving and reforming, they pearl,
promising hints of your lost beauty,
against the sky of a blank page.

horoscope

Today, the future will seem cold, full of thin ideas. Despite
the king's promise, constellations will keep closing.
Gemini: Resist your usual envy of animals: tigers and frogs,
unleashed from the parables of God. Unholy. Full of innocent sex.

A perpetual gray will keep inching toward you. Come closer, take
a sip from your life, what does it taste like? Try to embrace
this bewilderment. The new moon can prompt hope, but much
like your love-life, everything will turn on what isn't.

Today, your inner garden will ring a cacophonous green, yet death
will emerge from abstraction: heart and throat, blood and bone.
Prayers of angst, have never come so close to Uranus and Mars.
Lost friendships. The erotic indifference of the barista with lilac

hair will vanish into the quiet road to your house. Being can evade
nothingness no more. Not in the age of Aquarius. Not when
breath itself has become suspect. Don't try to sublimate grief into
flowers. Gemini, be brave. Accept. This suburban emptiness. Cold plate

of lunch. Base desires coiled up inside you. Tight fists of want. Books
stare you back. Sexual fantasies whet in dark. A semblance
of love. If only Venus moved through you. The expanse of your bed
might become bearable. Still warm. No remnants of smell, but your own.

kindness

A remembrance of trees and moods and
the melt of earth in rain.

Nostalgia stands at windows. Seaward.

Nothing in my past life fills me.
I have no desire to relive it.

I welcome this diminishing act:
On the balcony, I feel my life ebbing against

unexpected evenings. Sounds
of other people's children playing.

The woman in her see-through blouse, smoking.
Her melancholy perennial plants.

Last night, the old man upstairs lowered
a basket toward me. Two bottles of honey,

a book, and a note: *The hero is strangely close*

*to those who died young. Permanence does not
concern him.*

This morning on warm toast I spread
the darkwood syrup. Sweetness

broke through my tongue. I sat on the floor
and cried. Loneliness

is complete when we no longer understand
kindness.

to silence
> *after Rilke's To Music*

Silence: shadows of roads. Deeper:
silence of foreshadow. Our names there where all words
fade. Time
caught in memory's spire, memory
of the last hand held.

Grieve for what? This revolution
of grief to what end? for the smile of a moody God,
for the return of my mother, my ear on her pillowy breasts.

You forgotten friend: silence. In loneliness
your liberty, wide awake, magical. This space deep within us,
beneath the scent of ideas,
this holy wound
of modesty,
mortality.

Gathering sounds of night,
when the innermost point within us saturates,
and reaches to the outside, and from the bare edges of the world
beauty quietly returns:
still,
organic,
smelling of trees,
no longer habitable.

trees

She was alone when she made the nebula.
She made it from her own breath.
The arms of galaxies came out of her own arms.
One thing after the other she birthed:
clouds, oceans, blood, mouths, food, words.

Her sense of self dwindled.
She became numerous, infinitely dispersed
in spectrums of sand and rain.

But trees, she did not make with the intention
of *making*. They came out of her unobserved.
They were representations of her thoughts.
They could not move, but they knew her reasons.

They fed on the music of water-light.
Stoics, in gardens, protectors of empty roads
—cathedrals of her deepest-rooted dreams.

The first time a child touches a tree,
presses his ear on its bark, he can't let go.
Her secrets become immediate,
begin to circulate within him:

she jokes in moon-sheets and dew,
she laughs in lichen and ribbons of snow.

portrait of woman in see-through blouse

This is not the first time she has taken off her shirt
and caught me looking.

Intimacy is a gospel of secrets.

A bird hopped out of her cage,
a middle-aged faery about to escape,

then again, perhaps the entire alchemy is of smoke

from her cigarette—quickly rebuilding my past.

Her motherly breasts are bound to infest my sleep.

I ache to confess my most cherished sins.

Ivy keeps conquering the walls of her balcony,
in the foreground of evergreen blades:

her shoulders snare me in shame.

Birds trill in fields of water. Woman
of see-through blouse, her jeans one size too tight.

Amidst cloudy windows, in her proud eyes:
I am found, until the rain stops and she wipes

mascara from her cheek, murmuring

softly (what?) into the smell
of damp bricks. The fog of June returns.

Downstairs, a child wails for his mother,

and just like that, she is gone.

Tedium expands from the point of her departure.

Music tapers.

Poetry hides back into itself.
This: most ordinary, most banal of banalities
—burdens of life, return.

alter ego

Night after night
I see you from a passing train
in the diner of blurry windows,
through sharpening speed, I catch you
bathed in dim lights,
your slumped posture.

Why do you sit like that?
wearing a sweater mid-July,
your potential trapped in
empty rooms.

Night after night,
your reflection slides into me.

I wake up reeking of stagnant water,
disembodied, as if the hope of spring
and every color just poured
out of me—What is this place?

The farthest point from song, this
pale washed-out road, so distant
from the burst of birds or the sight of boats.

I try to give you a name
like the name of a wayside town where
no one stops, where trees remain small.

You are the picture of age,
without a familiar smell, a mild regret
I'm always trying to shed.

At the windless juncture of roads,
in your complexion no joy of success, nor
the courage of losing.

Fields on either side of you
flattening out to the sky, and in the middle
you again, my friend:

a balance of your own futility,
an involuntary equilibrium

of fatigue and light.

let me save you

Clocks have lost their pulse.

The hot morning retains mist.

Doors are open. Chairs are empty.
I sit on them, one after another.

A bee is retracing the path
of your scent—Were you really here?

It's found my arm: bright biblical wings,

my body awaits the relief of your sting.

By now, you must have reached the street
next to the bridge,

proudly walking toward your fragmentary career.

Oh, I don't have heart to tell you
about the omnipotence of the Ordinary—let it find you.

Beneath it all, earnest dear, there is only wind and flower
and abandoned bus stops.

I hope you miss your connection, come back.

Let me save you from this crisis
of confidence, from your ambition

to find your name in a world of cowards.

against form

Each morning I make my bed
to conquer chaos. A ritual to untangle

this always feeling unsafe, unloved, alone—
I make my bed to feel loved. I make it

with the child-like expectation of a stranger
coming in and saying:

Ah, now there's a well-made bed.
I do it to ward off despair, to exalt

the coordinates of my rest. To do something
with the mastery slowly diminishing

from my hands. So what, if wilderness
is the keeper of unity?

Once my bed is made, I take tea and read
by the window. That stubborn view of weeds,

how easily they have subdued
the clout of bricks. Coarsely toothed leaves,

—vigorously green. Through rain, snow, heat,
they persist. Against structure.

Tendrils. Without form.

Must acceptance reek of impotence?

tease

Don't do this.

These soothing words,
this distance, caffeinated lips,

take gin, swig hard, drink heat,
come undone for once.

Take the easy way out.

Be generous with your quality.

Blanket-like soft and inward, I imagine

where you sleep a ghostly music,
quiet roads, plants, autumnal waters.

And this distance: a secret, a celebration

until you, time will be sacred.
Days and minutes will be soft and curved.

Boredom: a mauve glistening loop,

milk of patience brightened
with wine.

Prayers for you are long and lithe.

Your ambivalence
comes up at dusk, shining in cups and keys

tender around the edges of summer heat
murmuring behind trees, and I, so purely alone

I know how to wait.

wrong side of bed

You wake up like a fish: flounder, common carp,
alone on a dry beach, because the tide's gone low and

the seawater—teeming with seals and octopi—
has withdrawn from you and your sickly flesh.

You wake up as a subtraction of friendship and spirit,

your gills gasp for rain from a sky blank and hot.

You wake up fatigued by visions of a shame that is
ancient, passed on to you

by generations of idolaters and adulterers, slanderers
and swindlers.

You wake up knowing that it was never you but God
who was unfaithful to you.

You wake up once again denied of heaven,

your gut eating itself—What to do

with all your knowledge of freshwater lakes and the Red Sea,

your comrades flying, frisking, racing through the Nile.

autumn

Wist rose into
the architecture of trees:

suspended meadow of oak, maple,
and birch quivered in cool wind

come from someplace of snow.

Green apples felled from
the sparse buildings of leaves.

Between branches: windows of dusk.

Before the slant of night: that golden
melancholy,

last berries, yellow bands
of flora, the atmosphere neared

combustion with visions of the life

we might have lived.

On the terraces of the forest
darkness leisurely drooped,

in the geometry of stars,
andromeda drew closer, paths

running up the slopes toward
the glimmer of town lay lost

in the crisp blackness
of pine.

wanderlust
for Ahmad

You opened like a new city, slowly
I saw your measure in shades,

behind you windows of almond bloom,
gates and pillars and a lilt of old tunes.

Everything I had done felt like a series
of subordinations toward you.

Between your shoulders the locket of glass, pain like this
cannot be healed by prayer.

Your sarcasm overwhelmed me.

I felt ashamed of my indelicate hands.

But you were bright on the terrace, reading, unperturbed
by the doves flying inordinately low.

Your eyes took what was once fugitive,
gave it permanence.

With you I still kept imagining being with you

in an old colonial hotel, in a room

with floating city views, our bodies full of sleep

and real dreams, and beyond us days

of clear skies, the excitement of undiscovered streets.

afternoon sun

This uninterrupted musical unit. One seeks respite.

How can white paint peeling off a balcony wall
be so simple and singularly painful?

Roads and rooms, be quiet. Let babies
be close to their mothers, let them have sleep.

Outside small trees sway like free verse
in hot air. Leaves keep breaking
innumerable moods of green.

The sky has never been so clear.

This post-lunch interlude: useless divinity
of cups and plates in the sink.

Men, idling behind office buildings,
lingering on a cigarette.

Under the afternoon sun,

every clerk is a poet,
every child a prophet.

When shades recede, and grief dapples
through harsh light—

ever so briefly, you grasp: the holy aimlessness

of mountains and riverbeds,
and ancient stars, heroes
of cafes and bars, and your beautiful fathers,
dying for nothing.

introvert

> *"Winter with its inwardness is upon us. A man is constrained to sit down, and to think."*
> —Henry David Thoreau

Maybe it is the fear of strangers.

This baptism of blankets: dark blinds shut,

untouched by morning, untouched by noon.

For an outside so fluid, to wish the inside concrete.

To be rocked by slow-moving, paradoxical dreams.

Mistful, woe-becalmed. Wind dispelling time.

To take comfort in the dimness of margins, this unsolvable,

incongruous night. The room retains its shadows.

To feel safe in the company of words,

draw from the textures of syntax a heat

never quite drawn from most people. Most people

only advancing your thirst as far

as a broken ladder, merely teasing,

tormenting, your mildewed breast

with tokens of weak light.

flirt

I don't want to flirt with you

by telling you of love or by making a sub-sexual joke.

I don't want to get drunk and lose my cool,

nor do I want to touch you, at least not in that way.

I want to touch you as one touches intangible things,

secretly, inside the supple bounds of thought. I don't mind

knowing your skin as mirrors know light. It is unbearable

enough when you leave, the whole city, the entire scheme

of life pursues me here—here in these rooms, where I read

Dostoevsky at night and begin to see his God.

And who's to say that lovemaking will be more maddening

than visualizing your jealous smile, or that the fable

you are now will not turn to unboxed dust

upon touch. No, I prefer you as a fruit in Plato's world

composed in Vermeer's hand. And I prefer myself as the joke

you won't understand. So be it, as most have said,

my addiction to distance and doubt. But what remains

between us let it have plurality of meaning.

Let it be a riddle: a self-annihilating word-game which

like your allure, once solved, shall cease to exist.

posture of embrace

Touch. Touch, my skin, as only angels
have touched: until the color of illness is lifted,
until it deepens no more, and I am free. Lighter

than mist, able again, to endure God's impossible love.

I walk back empty streets like a dog.
Earth smells stronger, if only, I had a tail I could swing
skyward, toward the abyss of dawn.

I come home, turn on the radio,
pour myself a glass of wine. A broadcast
of what overwhelms us, it continues: enormous
sadness. I make a sandwich I cannot eat.

Reclining on bed, in sleep everything is
rewombed: shelter.

I dream I'm a beetle, caught: within-without,
in a merciless noon. Beating for nectar
from tree trunks of feminine shapes.

I twist. No matter what, I am
in the posture of embrace. Waiting,

for her satin dress and greetings smelling of tea.
Oh, not because I know that happiness *is*.

My only true knowledge is hunger: vast,
whole, like mother's milk, I long

for a prophet.

nostos

Yesterday, the rösti you made,
it was sheer mouth-watering nostalgia

for a picnic at night, by the shore of a
black water lake and dots of light,
—a place I have never been.

When I say I am an old soul,
I'm afraid I'm being quite literal at that.

See, once I saw an ancient green carriage
drive past, horses and all, truly antique,
and I felt with great excitement

a strong kinship, as if I had once driven
it myself. The longing of nostalgia

is the feeling of being cheated, as if
something has been stolen from my own

past. It comes at odd hours, triggered
by voices in conversation, or images:

the eyes of an animal in headlights,
the smell of whiskey,
long winter coats.

In dreams, it goes even farther back in time:
to bygone cities, night after night,
I dream I am a scribe who's just

died in the Old Kingdom.

I watch them remove my organs with
the exception of my heart.

Rubbed with perfumed oil and
resins of plant, they glue strips
of linen around my limbs.

A pouch filled with smooth stones
is placed on my chest, symbols

of protection and rebirth are
painted with red and gold.

My pens, and inkpot, cakes of pigment,
are buried with me deep

in a necropolis, and I remain buried
until I wake to my phone blinking—
outside the window a hum

of rush hour traffic.
But in my skin, the whisper

of moonless wind round the tombs
of pharaohs, somehow remains.

Asnia Asim is the recipient of the University of Chicago's Humanities Fellowship and Brandeis University's Allan Slifka Award. Her poems have received multiple nominations for the Pushcart prize and Best of the Net Anthology and have appeared (are forthcoming) in *Typehouse, Michigan Quarterly, Cream City, The Rupture, Salamander, River Styx, Nimrod, Image, Juked,* and *BOOTH*, among others. Her work has been anthologized in *Halal If You Hear Me* (Haymarket Books). She's currently working on her forthcoming novel.

www.ingramcontent.com/pod-product-compliance
Lightning Source LLC
LaVergne TN
LVHW041603070426
835507LV00011B/1277